DATE DUE

NOV 5 '92		
7 '9?		
JAN 7 '93		
MAR 5 '93		
MAY 1 2 '93		
OCT 1 2 1993		
MAR 1 7 1994		
MAY 1 1 1994		
OCT 1 2 1994		
NOV 0 3 1994		
JAN 0 6 1995		
MAR 0 8 1995		
APR 1 9 1995		
MAY 1 8 1995		

CODES,
CIPHERS
AND
OTHER
SECRETS

KARIN N.
MANGO

CODES, CIPHERS AND OTHER SECRETS

FRANKLIN WATTS
NEW YORK | LONDON | TORONTO | SYDNEY | 1988
A FIRST BOOK

Library of Congress Cataloging-in-Publication Data

Mango, Karin N.
Codes, ciphers, and other secrets / Karin N. Mango.
p.   cm. — (A First book)
Bibliography: p.
Includes index.
Summary: Describes the many ways of hiding the real meaning of
what someone is trying to say by using a code or replacing the
message with a cipher.
ISBN 0-531-10575-X
1. Cryptography—Juvenile literature.   2. Ciphers—Juvenile
literature.   [1. Cryptography.   2. Ciphers.]   I. Title.   II. Series.
Z103.3.M36 1988
652'.8—dc10   88-5638 CIP AC

I am most grateful for
valued help from the following:
Madelyn Anderson, Renata Scheder,
Tony, Helen.
And, especially, Nick.

Illustrations by Vantage Art, Inc.

Photographs courtesy of:
The Bettmann Archive: pp. 13, 14, 68, 69, 74, 75, 78;
Culver Pictures: p. 16; New York Public Library
Picture Collection: p. 77; Humphries, Padden, and
O'Rourke: *A Basic Course in American Sign Language,*
copyright 1980, T.J. Publishers, Inc.: p. 79;
American Foundation for the Blind, Inc.: p. 81.

CONTENTS

CODES, CIPHERS AND OTHER SECRETS

CHAPTER ONE

ALL KINDS OF CODES

IIISSE AIWSAL ETTEOT
MFTFTS YTMTCE HLGTOH BTOOIZ

If you don't understand what this is, it's not surprising. It's secret.

1036 59 607 35 387 62

You may not be any clearer about this; it doesn't even use letters. It's secret too.

And this—it's not letters, it's not numbers, it's nothing familiar at all. But don't worry. The keys to these and many other secrets are here in this book.

The safest way to keep a secret is in your head with your mouth closed. In many situations, however, that is simply not possible. The examples above are other ways of keeping secrets. What they have in common is that they are hiding the real meaning of what they are saying by using a code or cipher. Although they are often taken for each other, codes and ciphers are quite different. In a code, each word or combination of words in a message is replaced by another word or combination, or by a number or symbol. In a cipher, each letter of the message is replaced by another letter, number, or symbol.

There are also other ways of keeping a message secret. You can use concealed writing—inserting your message in an otherwise ordinary-looking letter, for example. You can use invisible writing that can be made visible if you know how. Languages known only to the speakers are secret. You can also communicate secretly by using a visual, prearranged set of signals, or audibly, by listening to a prearranged code. You can create a code using touch alone.

There are also codes and ciphers that are *not* secret, like supermarket codes, social security numbers, semaphore signaling, the Morse code, and Braille, which is the system of writing for the blind.

The world is full of secrets that people try to keep hidden by using some kind of code or cipher. Governments—in war and peace—industry, business organizations, and special-interest groups have created and used ways of communicating their important, confidential information so that only those who are supposed to know can read and understand the message.

CHAPTER TWO

KEEPING SECRETS IN THE PAST

The need to keep important information secret goes back through all the years of recorded human history and even beyond, to the earliest communications between people. Codes and ciphers have been as important as weapons in war and as diplomacy in peace.

Ancient Egyptian hieroglyphics (pronounced hire-o-gliff-icks) were secret in a society where writing itself was not widespread and, therefore, like a code.

This is the word "Egypt" spelled out in hieroglyphics.

*The Greeks used the position of flames
to spell out coded messages.*

Ciphers have been used for plotting assassinations and the overthrow of governments. In the sixteenth century, Mary, Queen of Scots, used a cipher in her plans to assassinate Queen Elizabeth I of England and gain the throne for herself. The trouble was that her cipher was too easy—look at the example—especially for Elizabeth's canny secretary of state Walsingham. The plot was discovered, and it was fatal for Mary.

b g w m H ɔ f α γ   ρ k σ ω χ ∞ : Я b t   ⊥ ⊥⊥ Mⱼ o Iᵗ
A B C D E F G H I J K L M N O P Q R S T (U) V W X Y Z

Suspicious government officials in Renaissance Europe opened each other's mail, and resealed it after copying and deciphering, or solving, the contents. The government cipher-solving centers, dramatically called "black chambers," soon existed in most of Europe and have continued or been revived in one form or another ever since. Examples today are the GCHQ, the United Kingdom's code-breaking services, and the National Security Agency (N.S.A.) in the United States.

Couriers delivered and received secret messages personally until the invention of the electric telegraph, which was much used in the American Civil War. For the first time, information could be sent quickly over long distances; however, it was also instantly available to anyone who could tap the wires. The need, therefore, for codes and ciphers was urgent. Signal intelligence—monitoring and extracting information from various kinds of messages and signals—has been of the greatest importance since.

The invention of radio only intensified the need for codes and ciphers, since radio is also easy to intercept. Battles were won and lost in World War I through the skilled or clumsy use of codes and

A cipher machine captured from the Confederates in 1865

ciphers in those early days of radio. Weak codes or ciphers left their users vulnerable because the enemy could solve them.

Breaking the Zimmermann telegram code in World War I provided one of the chief reasons for America to enter the war. Arthur Zimmermann, the German foreign minister, sent a coded cable to Mexico suggesting an alliance against the United States. In victory, Mexico would regain its former territories of New Mexico, Texas, and Arizona. The cable was intercepted and solved by British Intelligence, and the United States was informed of its contents. The United States, unwilling until then to enter the war, changed its mind. This decision helped to determine the war's outcome in favor of the Allies.

In World War II, both sides recognized the supreme importance of code-making and code-breaking. *Purple* was the code name for the United States' reconstruction of a Japanese cipher machine. The machine enabled the United States to read many Japanese diplomatic messages. In the Atlantic, German U-boats (submarines) were able to sink large numbers of Allied ships because Germany had broken the British Merchant Navy code. When the British *Ultra* project broke the German U-boat cipher, code-named *Enigma,* the tables turned toward Allied victory.

Code names were popular in World War II—Purple, Enigma, Ultra. The Germans code-named the bombing of Coventry in England *Moonlight Sonata. The Manhattan Project* was the name for the Allied atom bomb plan, which ended the war.

Agents and spies used neutral code names like Chris and Jo, but also Cicero and even Washout. They carried coded means of identification, such as a particular magazine, agreed on in advance. They used code phrases to connect secretly by phone or in person with other agents. Disguise, anonymity, deception, and concealment were what they lived by. Agents, often young men challenged by "the Game" of spying and the danger, became more professional after World War I. After World War II, as teamwork and cipher machines took over, much of the individual, personal glamour and excitement seemed to disappear.

Today, the quantities of material being communicated have increased enormously. Great amounts of confidential information are sent around the world and stored in a vast array of computer systems. Decoding and deciphering also depend largely on computers and teams of specialized cryptanalysts—cipher-solvers. The bigger and more complex the network, the more vulnerable it is to break-ins and errors. There are, therefore, complex security systems and massive security problems. But if people are clever enough to access computers illegally in order to add, alter, or remove material, then other people will be clever enough to stop them. Access must be strictly limited to authorized personnel—those people who are supposed to be there. There must be frequent security audits, examining, checking, and verifying. And the way in must be barred by encryption—the use of codes and ciphers.

CHAPTER THREE

SECRET CODES

As we said earlier, most people are not aware of the difference between codes and ciphers and use the words interchangeably. The chances are that, before reading the first two chapters, you were one of those people. But now that you know the difference exists, you probably want to know more about both. After all, the definitions you read in chapter one were very brief, as definitions generally are. There is a lot more to tell about codes and ciphers and how they are used. So let's start by looking at codes in this chapter, and then go on to ciphers in chapters four through eight.

In a *code,* each *word or combination of words* in English is replaced by a *code word, number, phrase, or symbol.* Code-word groups can be longer or shorter than the words they stand for. A code may contain a great many words. As there is no consistent system of "translation," a code book is needed to keep track of all the meanings. Otherwise, it would be necessary to remember the meaning of every single code word.

In the *code book,* the entries are alphabetized for quick encoding (with the English words and phrases in alphabetical order) or decoding (with the code words in alphabetical order). You are *encoding* when you put words or combinations of words *into* code. You are *decoding* when you use the code book to get at the meaning of the message. Although the code-book entries are alphabetized, there is no internal logic to the code. This means that the meaning of an individual entry stands on its own; it is not related to the meaning of any other entry.

The point and beauty of codes is that they are fast and easy to use and can say a lot in a little space. For example, the code word DANCING might mean YOUR PRESENCE IS URGENTLY NEEDED.

You can create your own code book using symbols found in chapter eleven, or you may use made-up symbols, or words, phrases, or number groups.

You will need to make a copy for your partner, and maybe one or two copies for other friends. Of course, if any copy gets into the wrong hands, the whole setup will be worthless. For that reason, navy code books have for centuries been bound in lead. If a ship is about to be taken by the enemy, the code book is thrown into the sea, and the heavy lead carries it safely to the bottom. Since it lists all the meanings in a given code, a code book can be bulky, even without lead covers, and difficult to hide.

Codes are obviously very difficult to crack, since you have to know the meaning of most of the words. (Once you have enough meanings to understand the general idea of the message, you can usually supply the rest with common sense.)

An effective way to use codes is within sentences that look ordinary and innocent. An example: "You gave me a few particulars in your letter, but I should be obliged if you would go over it all again." But you know that "particulars" stands for MEET, "letter" for PARK, and "obliged" for THREE O'CLOCK.

Lord Baden-Powell was a British agent before World War I. (He was also the founder of the Boy Scouts.) He created ingeniously coded messages that looked perfectly innocent. Posing as an eccentric Englishman, a butterfly collector and artist, on the Dalmatian coast of Yugoslavia, he drew what appeared to be butterflies. But, as he describes it,

People did not look sufficiently closely into the sketches to notice that the delicately drawn veins of the wings were exact representations, in plan, of their own fort, and that the spots on the wings denoted the number and position of guns and their different calibers.

BOOK AND DICTIONARY CODES

Book and dictionary codes are both highly effective. In each case, sender and receiver must simply agree on which dictionary or which book to use. A code book is not required, just the book that has been chosen.

In a dictionary code, numbers are used to show the page and line on which a given word is to be found. The following example is taken from Webster's *New Collegiate Dictionary,* 1979 edition: 1036 59 607 35 387 62. The **boldface** words starting lines are the code words. This must be agreed on in advance between the code partners. The only problem is deciding which column is meant. The one that makes sense and is not gibberish is obviously right.

The decoded message is: SECRECY IS ESSENTIAL. You saw this example at the beginning of chapter one.

In a book code, numbers identify the page, line, and word for each word of the message. During the Revolutionary War, the great soldier and traitor, Benedict Arnold, offered to sell West Point, the strategic area on the Hudson River, to the British enemy. His letter was in a book code using a massive lawbook as the key. He found the message words in the lawbook and encoded by page, line, and word position. Words that were not in the lawbook, he mostly spelled out letter by letter using the same system. Arnold's recipient had only to know the title of the book. This code was time-consuming, tiresome, and impractical, but it was unbreakable.

CHAPTER FOUR

SECRET CIPHERS

As we said right at the beginning, the best place to keep something secret is in your head. That's not possible with most codes, but you can often do it with the kind of secret writing that codes are often confused with: ciphers. The origin of the word "cipher," by the way, is Arabic and means zero.

What codes and ciphers have in common is that only people with the key can understand the message. The difference is that in a code, each real *word* or combination of words is replaced by something else. In a cipher, each *letter* is replaced by another letter, number, or symbol. Most importantly, ciphers work by some kind of logical system.

There are two kinds of ciphers: transposition and substitution. This isn't as much of a mouthful as it sounds. In a *transposition* cipher, the *letters* of a plaintext—clear, intelligible—message *stay the same* but their *order is rearranged,* or transposed, using a specific method. All the letters of the plaintext message are always there.

In a *substitution* cipher, the *order stays the same,* but *each letter is replaced* by something else: it has something substituted for it.

You are *enciphering* when you substitute or transpose the letters of a message into a cipher. You are *deciphering* when you use the key to the cipher to uncover the meaning of a message. You are *cryptanalyzing* when you break the message down and solve it *without* having the key. The word deciphering is often used in both cases; it's all right to do so when there is no chance of the method being misunderstood.

Certain "tricks of the trade" can be used to make a secret message harder to crack. An enciphered text can be arranged in groups of five-letter "words", or four, or six, so that you can't guess the meaning from the length of the individual words. The average length of a word in English is four to five letters, so this is a good disguise.

Encipherers also add *nulls* to words, meaningless letters that are used to pad out the five-letter words—or whatever length has been decided on—and make them harder to guess. Nulls should not in themselves spell anything.

The whole message can be run together without spaces and without punctuation. Even a regular message in English seems a little like code when written this way:

THESEHIEROGLYPHICSEVIDENTLYHAVEAMEANING

Here are a few practical hints for when you are encoding or enciphering. Don't use an undersheet that can retain the impression of your writing. Someone could use it to reconstruct your secrets. Use lined or squared paper; it helps to keep things straight or in a grid. A pencil should be neither too sharp nor too blunt, so as not to mark through the paper or, on the other hand, be unclear. You will need an eraser; we all make mistakes. Destroy wastepaper carefully. Many secrets have been found in wastebaskets.

CHAPTER
FIVE

TRANSPOSITION
CIPHERS

Agility is important in transposition ciphers. You have to be able to go backwards and forwards, up and down, diagonally, and jump across spaces. The system in the acrobatics is what enables you to keep your balance and solve the cipher.

The simplest transposition ciphers to create are also the easiest to solve.

Th es eHie Rogl yphl cseVi den tLyh aV eaMe aning

If you look at the above cipher, you can see that the plaintext has been changed simply by rearranging the spaces, which are not between the words any more, but *in* them, and, also by inserting capitals at random. If you ignore the new spacing, the message reads:

THESE HIEROGLYPHICS EVIDENTLY
HAVE A MEANING

This is the same sentence we used in the last chapter.

This same message transposed into backward cipher looks like this:

GNINAEM A EVAH YLTNEDIVE
SCIHPYLGOREIH ESEHT

To read it, instead of going from left to right as usual, start at the right and go letter by letter to the left.

You can combine these easy ciphers to make them trickier: backwards with different spacing might look like this:

GNINA EMAEV AHYLT NEDIV
ESCIH PYLGO REIHE SEHTZ

The null Z has been added to make all the words the same length and, therefore, harder to guess.

PICKET FENCE

Another way of rearranging the plaintext is known as the "rail fence" or "picket fence", because of the way the cipher looks as you set it up. Say this is your message:

IF IT IS SYSTEMATIC WE SHALL
GET TO THE BOTTOM OF IT

91705

Count the letters and divide the total in half. (If there's an odd letter, just add a null at the end.) Write the letters of the message on two lines, one up, one down, next up, next down and so on with no spaces between the words, like this:

I I I S S E A I W S A L E T T E O T M F T
F T S Y T M T C E H L G T O H B T O O I Z

Note the null Z at the end.

Write out the top row of letters, followed by the bottom row:

IIISSEAIWSALETTEOTMFTFT-
SYTMTCEHLGTOHBTOOIZ

Divide the whole thing into groups of six-letter "words:"

IIISSE AIWSAL ETTEOT MFTFTS
YTMTCE HLGTOH BTOOIZ

That's the enciphered message—you saw it at the beginning of the book.

To decipher, divide the enciphered message in half. Take the first letter of the first half, I, then the first letter of the second half, F. Keep adding letters from the first and second halves till they are used up. Divide logically into words. The Z doesn't fit? Forget about it.

This is a quick cipher to do. Variations on the theme are easy. Take THIS SAMPLE IS SHORT and make a three-line picket fence, adding a null, Q this time, at the end.

```
T  S  M  E  S  R
H  S  P  I  H  T
I  A  L  S  O  Q
```

Enciphered, this is TSMESRHSPIHTIALSOQ.

The picket fence cipher is simply a matter of dividing the sum total of letters by a particular number. You can also, for example, divide a message by four:

```
T  A  T  O
A  N  R  P
K  E  A  Y
E  X  C  X
```

Read across the rows: TATOANRPKEAYEXCX. Or if you want to make it into "words:" TATO ANRP KEAY EXCX.

The decipherer only needs to know that you have used a division by four—or, to turn it around—a multiplication of 4 times 4. You have written the message vertically and transposed it into a horizontal cipher. It means TAKE AN EXTRA COPY.

You can also arrange the rows backwards. You start at the right side with your first vertical line and work to the left, but you still "read" the enciphered "words" from left to right in the normal way. The sentence RETURN TO NORFOLK looks like this:

```
O  N  R  R
L  O  N  E
K  R  T  T
Q  F  O  U
```

The next step makes it ONRR LONE KRTT QFOU.

You can make a diagonal version, arranging the message on a slant. For example, NO BASIS FOR AN INVESTIGATION looks like this:

```
N  O  A  S  A
B  S  F  N  E
I  O  I  S  G
R  N  T  A  I
V  I  T  O  N
```

starting in the top left corner and reading this way:

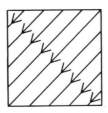

Or NOASA BSFNE IOISG RNTAI VITON.

CHAPTER
SIX

SUBSTITUTION
CIPHERS

"The devil himself cannot decipher a letter that is well written [in cipher]," said the Earl of Clarendon in 1659.

Substitution ciphers can be very hard to crack. Let's start with some easier ones!

NUMBER SUBSTITUTION

The most obvious substitution is to use numbers instead of the letters of the alphabet in the message. This is the basic idea: A=1, B=2, and so on. For example:

20 8 5 6 1 3 20 19 25 15 21 8 1 22 5 2 18 15
21 7 8 20 1 18 5 9 14 4 5 6 9 14 9 20 5

This, of course, takes exactly two minutes to crack:

THE FACTS YOU HAVE BROUGHT ARE INDEFINITE.

Make it a little harder: A=4, B=5 . . . W=26, X=1, Y=2, Z=3.
By a process of elimination, this doesn't take long to figure out either.

4 23 8 21 21 12 5 15 8 23 21 4 10 8 7 2

then becomes

A TERRIBLE TRAGEDY

ALPHABET SHIFT

Julius Caesar (ca 102 B.C.–44 B.C.) was one of the first people to
use an alphabet shift cipher. At its simplest, A becomes B, B becomes C, and so on until Z=A. Caesar's usual way was three letters
along so that A=D. Here's an example, broken up into five-letter
"words:"

LDPID PLOLD UZLWK DOOIR
UPVRI VHFUH WZULW LQJUU

Using the following key, this is how the cipher alphabet works out:

DEFGHIJKLMNOPQRSTUVWXYZABC: key
ABCDEFGHIJKLMNOPQRSTUVWXYZ: alphabet

The meaning, worked out, is:

I AM FAMILIAR WITH ALL FORMS OF SECRET WRITING

using two nulls at the end.

Using a key*word*—for example, SYMBOL—instead of a key *letter* as in D = A, you can make a much harder alphabet shift cipher. SYMBOL is a good word to pick because of the way the alphabet is used in the cipher. Print the keyword, which should not have any two letters the same, and follow it with the alphabet, leaving out the letters in the keyword as you come to them so that there are no repeats.

If you choose a keyword with letters near the beginning of the alphabet, once you have used up its letters, the rest of the alphabet will be the same in the plaintext and in the code. By choosing a word like SYMBOL with some letters at the end of the alphabet, the only duplicate will be Z, which looks like a cipher letter anyway:

SYMBOLACDEFGH I J KNPQRTU V WXZ: key
ABCDEFGH I JKLMNOPQRS TUVW X YZ: alphabet

Here is an example.

DMJIL OQQRC DQDQO IRDPO GXIOV RJHOZ

Deciphered, this reads: I CONFESS THIS IS ENTIRELY NEW TO ME.

You can do a keyword shift backwards too, starting at the Z end. Put the words in five-letter groups or alter the spacing between letters.

Instead of a key*word,* you can use a key *sentence* in a straightforward substitution using all the letters of the alphabet, like the familiar

THE QUICK BROWN F(O)X J(U)MPS: key
ABC DEFGH IJK L M N O P   QRS: alphabet

(O)V(E)(R) A L(A) Z Y D(O)G: key
    T   U V WX Y   Z: alphabet

As you can see, you write the alphabet underneath the key, skipping the repeated letters. Here is an example:

VKU SDSVUN KTS HUUF VX EXFEUTW T NUSSTCU
THE SYSTEM HAS BEEN TO CONCEAL A MESSAGE

Caesar's alphabet shift can be carried further. Divide the alphabet in half and put the second half below the first. The letters are now reciprocal. In other words, you get a double substitution: A = N and N = A, B = O and O = B, and so on.

GRID

Before Caesar, Polybius (ca 203 B.C.–ca 120 B.C.), a Greek historian, invented a substitution cipher using a grid or number box rather like this:

	1	2	3	4	5
1	A	B	C	D	E
2	F	G	H	I/J	K
3	L	M	N	O	P
4	Q	R	S	T	U
5	V	W	X	Y	Z

To encipher, each letter is represented by two numbers instead of one. You use the coordinates of the grid. First, take the number in the left-hand vertical column, and then take one from the horizontal line at the top of the box. The word CIPHER is enciphered this way: Find the C, which is at the junction of the 1 in the left-hand vertical column and the 3 in the horizontal one: 13. I is at the junction of 2 and 4: 24. The whole word enciphered is

$$13\ 24\ 35\ 23\ 15\ 42$$

Run the numbers together or make a longer message into groups of five-letter "words" and you have an impressive-looking cipher. To decipher, check each set of two numbers against the alphabet grid—starting with the left vertical column—and you have the plaintext letters back. To make it harder, shift the position of the letters: start with Z, for example, and move everything along one space.

OTHER
SUBSTITUTION CIPHERS

Using numbers and letters is only the tip of the iceberg in substitution ciphers. *Anything* can be substituted for the letters of the alphabet. How about this? You saw it right at the beginning of the book.

∨⊐L∨L ⊔⊐⌐ᒐ⌐·⊔∪∨L⌐·∨ ⊔∏·⌐⟩L∧ ⌐ ⌐L∨∨⌐⊐L

There seems no sense to this at all until you know the key:

AB	CD	EF
GH	IJ	KL
MN	OP	QR

To encipher, you draw the outline of the pattern next to the letters, showing the second letter in the group by an added dot. A is ⅃ , B is ∴⅃ and so on. The message reads:

THESE CHARACTERS CONVEY A MESSAGE

You can use the pattern in a variety of ways, so long as your friend knows the key. Again, this is a very old cipher, used by the Crusaders and written down by Giovanni Battista della Porta (1538–1615), an Italian who was an early writer on cryptography or secret writing. The cipher has been used by secret societies like the Freemasons and Rosicrucians, and the pattern may be familiar to you as the basis of tic-tac-toe. It is also known as the "pigpen" cipher because to soldiers using it in the Civil War the sections looked like one.

A number of household fixtures make excellent substitution ciphers. For example, the keys of a typewriter, including the signs for punctuation and machine control, can be effective when rearranged. The telephone dial can make an extended tic-tac-toe device. Since there is more than one letter and number for every hole or button, add a sign to show position.

The kitchen clock's numbers can be used for a cipher by arranging them in divisions of twelve or twenty-four or by position on the face. If your clock has Roman numerals, that could make a mysterious-looking cipher. All the shapes and symbols in chapter eleven can be used.

How about a musical cipher using notes, rests, and other musical symbols? The spy novelist, Bernard Newman, created one in a book about World War II. Every minim—♭—(long note) stood for one or more letters depending on its position in the lines and spaces of the staff. Other notes, creating a tune that included the minims, were just decorative padding.

In all these substitution ciphers, you do have to remember something—a group of letters, numbers, symbols, or pictures. But the remembering shouldn't be too difficult. The amount you have to remember is unlikely to be more than twenty-six: the number of letters in the alphabet.

CHAPTER SEVEN

HOW TO MAKE SOME CIPHERING GADGETS

If you like to make things, here are some opportunities. Alphabet shift ciphers can be used in a variety of combinations, using one alphabet (monoalphabetic) or several (polyalphabetic).

ST. CYR SLIDE

In the 1880s, the St. Cyr National Military College in France made a simple gadget to help in enciphering and deciphering shifts or "sliding" alphabets. A *St. Cyr Slide* is a *monoalphabetic* device—you only have to use one alphabet to decode it. This is how to make it:

You need two strips of fairly stiff paper (so it won't crumple easily). The first should be 6×1½ inches (15×4 cms.) long. Print the alphabet clearly along the top half of this strip. Carefully cut two identical vertical slits on the same strip, one below and slightly to the left of the A and the other below and slightly to the right of the Z, as shown in the diagram.

Cut the second strip of paper twice as long (12 inches or 30 cms.). It should also be cut just narrow enough to fit through the slits. Print the alphabet twice, one after the other, on this strip, using the same size lettering and spacing as before.

Slide the second alphabet through the slits, and any alphabet shift you want will appear in the window. For example, if L is your key, slide the movable alphabet along until L is under the A of the regular alphabet above. The rest of the shift cipher (on the movable strip) is now in place.

You can use this slide for twenty-six different alphabet variations—one for each letter of the alphabet. You can also make backward alphabet shifts or use numbers instead of letters, also going forwards or backwards. You can also make letter/number combinations or use symbols.

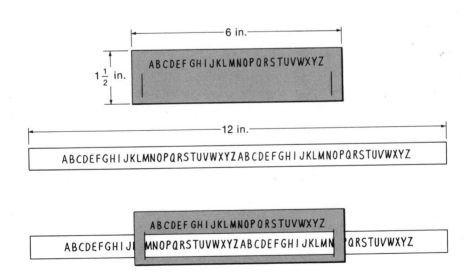

CIPHER WHEEL

A *cipher wheel* is basically a St. Cyr slide curved round until Z meets A in a circle. To make one, you need a pencil, a sheet of light cardboard (the backing of a yellow legal pad is good), a compass, ruler, scissors, and a metal paper fastener.

Draw a circle near the top of the cardboard with the compass set at three inches (7½ cms.). This makes a six-inch circle (15 cms.). Draw a second circle lower down the cardboard with the compass set at 2½ inches (6½ cms.), making a five-inch circle (12¾ cms.). Cut both circles out carefully.

Print the letters of the alphabet as evenly spaced as you can round the edge of the smaller wheel, as shown in the diagram. Divide the letters more clearly by drawing a line with the ruler between each letter to the center of the circle—marked by the pinpoint hole the compass made.

Attach the smaller wheel on top of the larger one with the paper fastener. Around the edge of the larger wheel, exactly opposite the letters of the smaller wheel, print another regular alphabet (or a cipher alphabet of your choice, or a random scrambling of the letters. Symbols or numbers can also be used on the outer wheel).

Decide on the key letter of your cipher on the outside wheel—say, P. Turn it until it reaches the A of the regular alphabet on the smaller wheel and the cipher is ready.

To encipher, using the message THE RULES GUIDE US, find the first message letter in the inner, fixed circle and write the corresponding letter shown on the outer, movable circle. For example, using key letter P:

I W T G J   A T H V J X S T J H

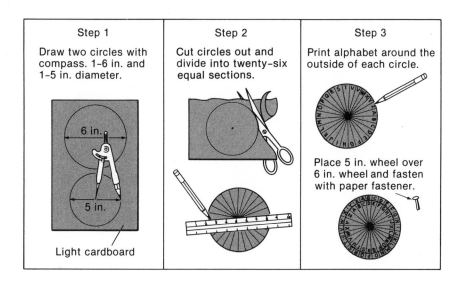

Step 1	Step 2	Step 3
Draw two circles with compass. 1-6 in. and 1-5 in. diameter.	Cut circles out and divide into twenty-six equal sections.	Print alphabet around the outside of each circle.

6 in.

5 in.

Light cardboard

Place 5 in. wheel over 6 in. wheel and fasten with paper fastener.

Cipher Wheel

To decipher, look for the letter I in the outer, turning, circle and write the letter shown in the inner, fixed circle, T, and so on, so that eventually the message reads:

THE RULES GUIDE US

This is the simplest version of a cipher wheel. To make a harder cipher, a *polyalphabetic* one, decide with your partner in advance on the beginning key, say L=A. Set your wheels at L=A. Look for the first letter of your message on the regular alphabet wheel and write the cipher letter shown opposite it. Then move the outer wheel clockwise one or more spaces the way you have also agreed on in advance. Look for the next letter of the message and write its cipher equivalent shown opposite. Again move the outer wheel clockwise for as many spaces as the first time. Repeat the shift for the third letter of the message, and so on. Each movement of the wheel enciphers a message letter in a new cipher alphabet. Here is an example using L = A as the first key and moving one space clockwise after each letter of the message:

N Y W K L G Q Q H U T A F C

To decipher, you only have to know the beginning key (L = A in this case) and how many spaces you should move the outer wheel clockwise after each letter of the message (one space in this example). The deciphered message reads:

CONCEAL MESSAGE

This cipher takes a while to do, even with a cipher wheel, but just because it is more difficult, it is effective.

Cipher wheels go back a long way. One of the earliest was made by a versatile Italian poet/painter/philosopher/musician/architect called Leon Battista Alberti (1404–1472). He used two different-sized copper discs as his wheels.

Perhaps the most familiar creator of one of these machines was Thomas Jefferson. Apart from his talents as soldier and statesman, Jefferson was a gifted inventor and scientist. Jefferson's cipher wheel had as many as thirty-six alphabet wheels on a central shaft. In 1891, Etienne Bazeries, a French cryptographer, made a cipher machine of twenty alphabets based on Jefferson's. This became one of the cornerstones of today's very complex polyalphabetic cipher machine systems.

VIGENÈRE CIPHER

Here is a famous polyalphabetic cipher for which you will only need paper and pencil. It is called the Vigenère cipher after Blaise de Vigenère, a French cryptographer of the sixteenth century, although the idea goes back to Caesar.

Choose a keyword with no repeating letters, maybe SYMBOL again. Write it above the letters of your message—for example, HAVE CONFIDENCE—again and again until you come to the end of the message and every message letter has a corresponding key letter. It doesn't matter if the keyword is incomplete at the end:

    S Y M B O L S Y M B O L S Y
    H A V E C O N F I D E N C E

That's the quick part.

Now you need a large sheet of paper to draw a table with twenty-six alphabets. Don't panic. If you use squared or graph paper and follow the diagram, it will be easy and neat. Just notice that each alphabet starts with the letter after the one before; that is, the first alphabet goes A to Z, the second, B through the alphabet to A again, the third starts with C and goes through to B, and so forth.

Outside the grid, print the alphabet once more along the top and once down the left side.

To start enciphering, find the key letter (from the keyword SYMBOL) above the first message letter: S. Find this key letter in the vertical left side alphabet outside the grid. Find the first letter of the message above the top, horizontal alphabet outside the grid: H. Follow both lines along until they intersect: Z. This is the first letter of your cipher.

Use the same method with every letter of the plaintext message. Your partner needs to know the keyword and draw the same grid:

Plaintext Letter

	A	B	C	D	E	F	G	H	I	J	K	L	M	N	O	P	Q	R	S	T	U	V	W	X	Y	Z
A	A	B	C	D	E	F	G	H	I	J	K	L	M	N	O	P	Q	R	S	T	U	V	W	X	Y	Z
B	B	C	D	E	F	G	H	I	J	K	L	M	N	O	P	Q	R	S	T	U	V	W	X	Y	Z	A
C	C	D	E	F	G	H	I	J	K	L	M	N	O	P	Q	R	S	T	U	V	W	X	Y	Z	A	B
D	D	E	F	G	H	I	J	K	L	M	N	O	P	Q	R	S	T	U	V	W	X	Y	Z	A	B	C
E	E	F	G	H	I	J	K	L	M	N	O	P	Q	R	S	T	U	V	W	X	Y	Z	A	B	C	D
F	F	G	H	I	J	K	L	M	N	O	P	Q	R	S	T	U	V	W	X	Y	Z	A	B	C	D	E
G	G	H	I	J	K	L	M	N	O	P	Q	R	S	T	U	V	W	X	Y	Z	A	B	C	D	E	F
H	H	I	J	K	L	M	N	O	P	Q	R	S	T	U	V	W	X	Y	Z	A	B	C	D	E	F	G
I	I	J	K	L	M	N	O	P	Q	R	S	T	U	V	W	X	Y	Z	A	B	C	D	E	F	G	H
J	J	K	L	M	N	O	P	Q	R	S	T	U	V	W	X	Y	Z	A	B	C	D	E	F	G	H	I
K	K	L	M	N	O	P	Q	R	S	T	U	V	W	X	Y	Z	A	B	C	D	E	F	G	H	I	J
L	L	M	N	O	P	Q	R	S	T	U	V	W	X	Y	Z	A	B	C	D	E	F	G	H	I	J	K
M	M	N	O	P	Q	R	S	T	U	V	W	X	Y	Z	A	B	C	D	E	F	G	H	I	J	K	L
N	N	O	P	Q	R	S	T	U	V	W	X	Y	Z	A	B	C	D	E	F	G	H	I	J	K	L	M
O	O	P	Q	R	S	T	U	V	W	X	Y	Z	A	B	C	D	E	F	G	H	I	J	K	L	M	N
P	P	Q	R	S	T	U	V	W	X	Y	Z	A	B	C	D	E	F	G	H	I	J	K	L	M	N	O
Q	Q	R	S	T	U	V	W	X	Y	Z	A	B	C	D	E	F	G	H	I	J	K	L	M	N	O	P
R	R	S	T	U	V	W	X	Y	Z	A	B	C	D	E	F	G	H	I	J	K	L	M	N	O	P	Q
S	S	T	U	V	W	X	Y	Z	A	B	C	D	E	F	G	H	I	J	K	L	M	N	O	P	Q	R
T	T	U	V	W	X	Y	Z	A	B	C	D	E	F	G	H	I	J	K	L	M	N	O	P	Q	R	S
U	U	V	W	X	Y	Z	A	B	C	D	E	F	G	H	I	J	K	L	M	N	O	P	Q	R	S	T
V	V	W	X	Y	Z	A	B	C	D	E	F	G	H	I	J	K	L	M	N	O	P	Q	R	S	T	U
W	W	X	Y	Z	A	B	C	D	E	F	G	H	I	J	K	L	M	N	O	P	Q	R	S	T	U	V
X	X	Y	Z	A	B	C	D	E	F	G	H	I	J	K	L	M	N	O	P	Q	R	S	T	U	V	W
Y	Y	Z	A	B	C	D	E	F	G	H	I	J	K	L	M	N	O	P	Q	R	S	T	U	V	W	X
Z	Z	A	B	C	D	E	F	G	H	I	J	K	L	M	N	O	P	Q	R	S	T	U	V	W	X	Y

Key Letter

S Y M B O L S Y M B O L S Y
H A V E C O N F I D E N C E

then becomes

Z Y H F Q Z F D U E S Y U C

To decipher, write the keyword over and over the cipher text:

S Y M B O L S Y M B O L S Y
Z Y H F Q Z F D U E S Y U C

The letter above the first cipher letter is S. Find it in the vertical left-hand column outside the grid. Move along horizontally until you reach the first cipher letter, Z. Move up vertically until you reach the regular horizontal alphabet outside the grid: H, which is the first letter of the message. Repeat for each letter and you get

HAVE CONFIDENCE

Of course, if you don't know the keyword, it's a whole other story and very complex. You may need the National Security Agency to help you with that.

Extra complications can be introduced to foil would-be code-breakers. An "influence" letter can interrupt the keyword, which then has to start from the beginning again. For example, in the phrase THE FIRST MESSAGE SUBMITTED TO ME, if the influence letter is I, each time I appears the keyword has to start again, like this:

    S Y M B S Y M B O L S Y M B O L S Y M S Y M B O L S Y M
    T H E F I R S T M E S S A G E S U B M I T T E D T O M E

Or a text can be used as a key, say the first words of Genesis in the Bible. Or the alphabet can be scrambled. Or . . .

SKYTALE

There's one more gadget, this time for a transposition cipher using all the letters of the plaintext message. It's called a skytale (pronounced skit-a-lee) and was used by the Greeks about 500 B.C. The word means "staff"; a Greek general's staff, or stick, was used in

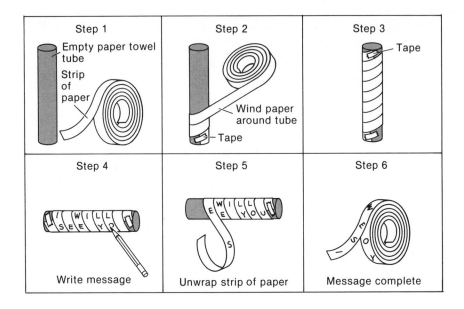

Step 1	Step 2	Step 3
Empty paper towel tube Strip of paper	Wind paper around tube Tape	Tape
Step 4	Step 5	Step 6
Write message	Unwrap strip of paper	Message complete

constructing and deciphering the messages sent between commanders in battle. The idea is simple: a scroll rolled round a pole. It even rhymes.

To make a skytale, you need an empty paper-towel tube (the staff) and a long, narrow strip of paper (the scroll), both of them about one inch (2½ cms.) wide and four to five feet (120 to 150 cms.) long. You also need a pencil and some tape.

Tape the end of the strip to the bottom of the tube and carefully wind it round and round the tube until you reach the top, as in the diagram. Tape this end of the paper strip to the top of the tube.

Print the message across the length of the tube, one letter on each row of the paper strip, turning the tube when you need to start a new line. Carefully remove the tape. Unroll the message, which is now a strip of scrambled letters. Only when your friend uses an identical tube (staff) to roll the strip (scroll) up again, will the message reappear, for example,

I HAVE IN FRONT OF ME THESE PRODUCTIONS

CHAPTER EIGHT

SOLVING CIPHERS

Creating ciphers is only half the story. What if you find this message written in blood on a scrap of paper and stuffed through a crack in your school locker?

> WKH HADPSOHV DUH DOO WDNHQ IURP WKH
> DGYHQWXUH RI WKH GDQFLQJ PHQ

Cryptanalysis—solving ciphers without having a key—requires paper, pen and pencil, and patience. It means working out the steps logically and carefully. You may not get the right answer the first time and have to start again at square one, but once you have the idea, it does go quite fast. Common sense and intuition are also assets. Unless the message uses very strange words or subject matter, the common-sense choice is likely to be right . . . most of the time.

The main thing to remember is that ciphers work on a system, and once you have grasped the system you've got the cipher.

There are some basic "tools" available to help you, the cryptanalyst. Every language has a characteristic structure. Grammar and word order help first of all to show which language is being used. In German, for example, the verb goes at the end of the sentence. Then there is the frequency with which certain letters and letter combinations are used—as well as combinations that are *not* used. For example, *ao* is a word ending in Portuguese; *shch* is a combination of letters you sometimes find in Russian words when transliterated (written out) in the Roman (instead of Cyrillic) alphabet. Neither "ao" nor "shch" is used in English. Q is followed by U in English and no English word ends in Q, but in transliterated Arabic words, the opposite is true, as in the place names Qatar and Iraq. No English word ends with J and few with V, Z, I, X, U, C, or B.

Subject matter is a clue. If you have the context, or can guess it—military, sports, comics—you can make educated guesses at the words of the message.

The main tool is a *letter frequency table.* That is, the average number of times a letter appears in an average text. If you can discover which letters are most frequently used and compare your message with the frequency table, you are on your way to solving it.

The commonest letter in English is E (as it is in French, German, Spanish, and Italian—in Russian, on the other hand, it is O). The next is T. If you can find which are the T's and E's in the message, you have already solved a quarter of it! E is also the most common ending letter and T the most common beginning letter of words in English. The table—"toolbox"—on pages 50–52 is for you to refer to when you are solving ciphers. It shows the order of frequency, *starting with the most common.*

Letter frequency:

E T A O N R I S H D L F C
M U G Y P W B V K X J Q Z

The five *most frequently used consonants*—T N R S H—
make up a third of most messages. And the first nine letters of this list make up nearly three-quarters of most messages.

A letter standing alone is most probably A or I.
The consonant most often followed by a vowel is N.

Pairs of the *same* letters:

LL EE SS OO DD TT FF RR
NN PP CC MM GG BB VV ZZ

RR is most often used in the middle of a word—e.g., ba*rr*ier.
SS is most often used at the end of a word—e.g., sweet-
ne*ss*.

Pairs are often in *patterns:*

NOON, cOMMOn, bOTTOm,
bARRAge, mISSIon, mILLIon

Pairs of *different* letters:

TH HE AN RE ER IN ES ON EA TI AT EN

TH is most often used at the beginning of a word. ER is
most often used at the end of a word. H at the end of a
word is often preceded by: G—e.g., enouGH; T—e.g.,
tooTH; C—e.g., touCH; S—e.g., buSH.

In two-letter words with I, the I is always first, e.g., IN. In two-letter words with E, the E is always second, e.g., BE. O is the most common letter in two-letter words.

Most common *two-letter words:*
OF TO IN IT IS BE AS AT
SO WE HE BY OR ON DO IF

Groups of *three* letters:
THE ING AND ION ENT

Most common *three-letter words:*
THE AND FOR WAS HIS NOT BUT
YOU ARE HER HAD ALL ONE

Common three-letter words
ending with *pairs* of letters:
ALL SEE BEE FEE ADD ODD TOO EBB EGG ILL

Common three-letter words
beginning and *ending*
with the *same* letter:
DAD MUM EYE POP GAG NUN DUD SOS

Most common *four-letter words:*
THAT WILL HAVE WILL YOUR
THIS FROM THEY KNOW

Most common four-letter ending:
-TION

Watch for four-letter words that are three-letter words plus S for plural.

Words most often *start* with:

T A O M S W B C D F R H I
Y E G L N P U J K V Q X Z

Some experts put O before A in this list and M tenth.

Most common *second* letter in a word:

H O E I A U N R T

Most common *third* letter:

E S A R N I

Words most commonly *end* with:

E T D S N R Y F L O G H A K M P U W

More than half of all English words end in E, T, D or S.

Most common word *ending combinations:*

ING NCE ENT ION

G at the end of a word is usually part of -ING.

Commonest words:

AND, THE

The average length of a word in English is 4 to 5 letters. Remember that many ciphered messages are purposely divided into four- or five-letter "words."

SOLVING CIPHERS

You now have a lot of information. Here's the cipher message again:

WKH HADPSOHV DUH DOO WDNHQ IURP WKH
DGYHQWXUH RI WKH GDQFLQJ PHQ

Copy the cipher message onto a piece of paper to work with. It is generally not a good idea to work on the cipher message itself, as one makes mistakes and then the whole thing can become a mess and you can't tell where you are. Use a pen for the message and a pencil for deciphering; it's easier to see what you are doing.

First, you have to decide if you have a transposition or a substitution cipher. If the message is in some kind of symbol, you would know it was almost certainly a substitution. With symbols, if not obvious like the pigpen, you treat them as letters: the most frequently used symbol is likely to stand for E and so on.

If a message is in letters, it is also easy to decide. Make a frequency table of all the different letters used in the message, putting a mark next to each letter every time it occurs in the message:

W	IIIII	N	I
K	III	Q	IIIII
H	IIIIIIIIII	I	II
A	I	R	II
D	IIIIII	G	II
P	III	Y	I
S	I	X	I
O	III	F	I
V	I	L	I
U	III	J	I

If your message list is basically similar to the frequency list in the chart above—lots of E's, T's, A's, O's, N's, and S's, a lot of vowels—you probably have a transposition cipher. The letters of ordinary English have been used and just rearranged in some way. We'll work one of these out later in this chapter. The ciphered message in the example above is obviously not a transposition cipher. It looks like a substitution cipher. You just have to hope it turns out to use normal English grammar.

It's lucky that it is relatively long. Short substitution cipher messages are often very hard to solve for the simple reason that they don't have enough letters. You have to work without any elbow room. A short message can be quite *un*average. For example, the sentence LOOK FOR UNUSUAL SYMBOLS has no E's or T's at all. It would be hard to work on this message if it were enciphered. The "best" messages are at least 50 letters long.

The commonest letter of the cipher message—H—is probably E. Write each letter as you discover it next to its cipher equivalent in your frequency chart. Wherever an H occurs in your copied cipher, put an E above it.

W or D in the message could be T. With E at the end of a three-letter word, it is likely to be THE. Therefore, K in the cipher is H, a bonus for you.

Q and D in the message are the next most common letters. Try them for A, O, or N. Q can't be O; no English word ends in EO. A is unlikely, so try Q for N. Then D for A. Okay.

How about trying to place the O? Try cipher letters P and U for it. They don't work. You would have E-AO--E- in the second word and AOE in the third one. Forget it for the moment and try a totally different tack: TA-EN can only be TAKEN.

This is the message so far:

```
      THE E A   E A E A   TAKEN
      WKH  HADPSOHV  DUH  DOO  WDNHQ

         THE A  ENT   E   THE
      IURP WKH DGYHQWXUH RI WKH

             AN   N   EN                    ˛
             GDQFLQJ PHQ
```

TAKEN could be followed by FROM? Try it. If so, you have the meaning of the letters I, U, R, P. Fill them in. And you now have O without even trying.

    There's a three-letter word with the last two letters repeated: DOO. The most common pair is -LL. ALL. Okay again.

    The next commonest single letter in English is D. Does G stand for D? Probably.

    This is the message now:

```
      THE E AM LE  ARE ALL TAKEN
      WKH HADPSOHV  DUH  DOO  WDNHQ

      FROM THE AD ENT RE OF THE
      IURP WKH DGYHQWXUH RI  WKH

             DAN   N MEN
             GDQFLQJ PHQ
```

55

And now you have about enough information to fill in the remaining letters. Deciphered, the message reads:

THE EXAMPLES ARE ALL TAKEN FROM
THE ADVENTURE OF THE DANCING MEN

That's a story about Sherlock Holmes, the great detective created by Sir Arthur Conan Doyle.

The cipher was a regular D = A Caesar shift. Well . . . maybe it was red ink, not blood, on the scrap of paper.

How about this?

OVEARECDYSTEQTIT

Do a quick check that it is not a simple backwards cipher or a space rearrangement. No? Make a frequency chart: three E's, two T's, the rest of the letters occur only once. It is a short message, but it has a more or less normal frequency. As Q is without a U, it might well be a null. This is most likely a transposition cipher. In chapter 5, you saw how these were based on various multiples. In deciphering, you have to find which multiplication was used, and whether it was forward, backward, or even diagonal. That can be a long, slow process, as the only way is to try all the possible combinations.

The ciphered message is sixteen letters long. In transposition ciphers, the length—or shortness—of a message is unimportant; in fact, a short one makes solving easier as there are fewer choices. You can make 16 by multiplying 8×2, 2×8, or 4×4. So there are only three main choices, unless there are further complications such as the words not being in the correct order.

Let's try 2 × 8 first; that is, a two-line picket fence. That produces OYVSETAERQETCIDT, which is nonsense.

Eight by two gives eight very short lines. Reading down the two columns is again nonsense:

OV

EA

RE

CD

YS

TE

QT

IT

We are left with 4 × 4. Keep your fingers crossed. Write the message out in four vertical lines of four letters each and read down each column:

O R Y Q

V E S T

E C T I

A D E T

Not this way. Try setting up the rows horizontally and reading down:

O V E A

R E C D

Y S T E

Q T I T

It doesn't work if you read the vertical rows from left to right, but words *do* appear as you scan down the columns from right to left. The message reads:

A DETECTIVE STORY

And the Q is a null. This is a backward transposition cipher.

CHAPTER NINE

SECRET AND CONCEALED WRITING

INVISIBLE WRITING

Sometimes you want your writing to be secret without using codes or ciphers. The most secret way of all is invisible writing, for the simple reason that it can't be seen. Secret writing uses invisible ink. The idea goes back at least to the Roman naturalist, Pliny the Elder (ca 23 A.D.–79 A.D.). Invisible inks have been used for intelligence since the Renaissance.

In the American Revolution, George Washington told off his intelligence chief for sending him a "blank" paper written in a "sympathetic stain" of invisible ink. "A better way," Washington said, "is to send a letter with some mixture of family matters and between the lines communicate with the stain the intended intelligence." In other words, make it look innocent.

For secret writing, you need either an old-fashioned pen with a metal nib, an old fountain pen, a watercolor paintbrush, or a toothpick. You can also use a feather quill from your pet peacock! Don't press hard if using something pointed, as you will leave suspicious marks on the "empty" paper.

Food ingredients are the simplest, safest, and best "inks:"

MILK

LEMON JUICE (or ORANGE or GRAPEFRUIT)

APPLE JUICE

VINEGAR

ONION JUICE (onion tears only temporary)

COCA COLA or PEPSI COLA (or other soft drinks; dilute
   slightly with water)

SUGAR (dissolve one teaspoon in a cup of water)

Use milk on hard paper like good typing paper. The other "inks" are best on more absorbent paper. Lined paper will help you keep lines straight and not write over your own invisible writing.

To make the writing visible, heat the paper gently above a toaster or against a 60 or 75 watt bulb. Or heat gently with a warm iron—unplugged. No need to use matches or an open flame, as you might burn the paper (lost writing) or yourself (painful). In fact, it is a good idea when using any of these heating methods to have an adult nearby—but not peeking.

You can use chemical substances for inks. Here are a few:

SALT—you probably have it at home.

EPSOM SALTS (magnesium sulfate)—buy this at a drugstore.

BAKING SODA (sodium bicarbonate)—you can get this at the supermarket or grocery store.

To use each of these, dissolve one teaspoon in a cup of water. You can "bring them back" with heat, same as the others.

IRON SULFATE

Buy the smallest amount the drugstore will sell you, as it lasts a long time. Then, at the supermarket, buy washing soda (sodium carbonate). Dissolve ¼ teaspoon iron sulfate in ¼ cup of water. To read back, dissolve ½ teaspoon washing soda in ¼ cup of water, dip a cotton ball or Q-tip into the mixture, and touch the writing. Don't taste!

An unusual kind of secret writing is to write on a hard-boiled egg with a mixture of one ounce alum to a pint of vinegar. When the egg is shelled, the message is visible on the egg itself. Alum, a white crystalline compound, can be bought at the drugstore. It's not poisonous, but again, don't taste it!

Experiment until you are satisfied with your secret writing, then send a message to a pre-warned friend. As General Washington suggested, write the invisible message between the lines of a regular letter.

The trouble with invisible writing is that once it is reconstituted, it's there for everyone to see. Make sure it's the right moment.

CONCEALED WRITING

People have been hiding messages for as long as there have been messages to hide. Secret agents use a "drop" for messages to be deposited or collected; maybe in a rotted tree stump or behind a movable brick in a wall. You can do the same. Just remember to protect the message from the weather or animals. The Russian master spy, Rudolf Abel, used a hole in some steps in a Brooklyn park. This drop was discovered when the Parks Department started repair work and found the hole.

Agents often conceal messages on themselves, in a hollowed-out shoe heel, for example, or even a hollowed-out tooth. During the Boer War in South Africa, a message was sent between two officers in a walking stick with a plugged hole for the message. You can padlock a secret message in a closet or box and give a key only to your friend.

An effective kind of concealed writing is called the Cardano–Richelieu grille, after the two chief inventors. Geronimo Cardano (1501–1576), an Italian physician, mathematician, and astrologer, used individual letters for his grille. Cardinal Richelieu (1585–1642), Louis XIII's chief minister, used words in his version. The idea is simple.

You need two sheets of firm paper and one of ordinary paper. Tape one piece of firm paper over the other: this is to make an identical copy for your partner. Decide on a short message using fairly ordinary words. For example: WHAT ONE MAN CAN INVENT ANOTHER CAN DISCOVER. Write it spaced randomly on the third sheet of paper, as in the diagram. Place this sheet over the taped ones. Outline the position of the words by making a rectangle round them with the sharp point of a pair of scissors. This should show through to the under sheets. Cut out the rectangles in both the sheets at the same time.

Fill up the space on the page with a chatty letter including the message words as naturally as possible. When your partner receives the message, the sheet with the holes is placed over the letter and the secret message appears in the holes. This message is somewhat odd, but then it was written by Sherlock Holmes.

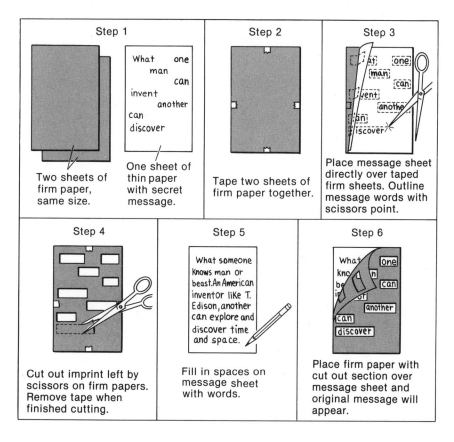

Step 1

What one
man can
invent
another
can
discover

Two sheets of firm paper, same size.

One sheet of thin paper with secret message.

Step 2

Tape two sheets of firm paper together.

Step 3

Place message sheet directly over taped firm sheets. Outline message words with scissors point.

Step 4

Cut out imprint left by scissors on firm papers. Remove tape when finished cutting.

Step 5

What someone knows man or beast. An American inventor like T. Edison, another can explore and discover time and space.

Fill in spaces on message sheet with words.

Step 6

What one
kno man can
be or
if another
can
discover

Place firm paper with cut out section over message sheet and original message will appear.

Cardano–Richelieu Grille

Marking newsprint is another way to conceal a message. Agree on a section of the newspaper with a friend. Think of your message. Make a tiny dot or a pinprick under the first letter of your message the first time it appears on the newspaper page. Go on "reading" and look for the first appearance of the second letter; put another dot or pinprick, and so on for the whole message.

To make it harder—perhaps someone else will notice the pencil marks or the pinholes—tell your friend the message is the letters immediately *after* the dot. Even harder: encipher the message first and *then* use the dot or pinprick method.

Dots of a different kind are used in microdot hidden writing. This is a photographic method that miniaturizes a message into, literally, something the size of a dot, like the period at the end of this sentence. The receiver has to know where the dot is planted in an innocent text and then he or she magnifies it for reading. An analogy is the "burst transmission" method of condensing a spoken message into a fraction of the time it took to say it. Governments often encipher messages before using microdot photography.

You can miniaturize your own writing. Tiny handwriting looks like a cipher, or is simply too much trouble for someone else to bother with, but it shouldn't be so small you can't read it back yourself.

CHAPTER TEN

SECRET LANGUAGES

Writing in code or cipher, hiding messages, using computers or other machines for communication: in all these methods, something has been conspicuously absent—the human voice. In nearly all these systems, the mouth has been firmly closed.

USING REAL LANGUAGES

There is another secret world of *spoken* languages, when people are together and cannot or do not want to speak openly. They can use a language unknown to the others present. If you and your friend speak Spanish and no one else in your group does, you have, in effect, a secret language. But a great many people do know Spanish and so you can't be certain that your conversation is as secret as you think.

In the past, in some countries, French was the "secret" language of a small, powerful aristocracy. This was true in England after the Norman Conquest, at European courts, and in nineteenth-century pre-revolutionary Russia.

In early and medieval Europe, monks and other scholars communicated in Latin, a language unknown by the rest of the mostly illiterate population. If you learn Latin at school, you may be able to use it as a secret language. This is a "dead" language; that is, it is no longer spoken today. Another is Anglo-Saxon, spoken and written in England between 650 and 1100 A.D. Scholars have reconstructed how it sounded, and many of the letters look familiar. The ones that aren't are different enough to make a good coded language. This is the Anglo-Saxon alphabet:

```
  a  æ  b  c  d  e  f  ʒ  h  i     l  m  n  o  p     r  s  t  þ  ð  u     þ     y
(car)(fat)
```

```
A A B C D E F G H I (J K) L M N O P (Q) R S T th th U (V) W (X) Y (Z)
                                                  /    \
                                               start  elsewhere
                                               of word in word
```

There are many living languages spoken by relatively few people. You are not very likely to be understood if you speak Icelandic, for example, or Irish, outside the countries where it is spoken.

If you are a native American, you may know an American Indian language. That's as near secret as possible, because most of these languages were not even written down until quite recently. American Indian languages, such as Choctaw and Chippewa, were tested for use as secret languages for transmitting messages in World War II, but Navajo, which is extremely complex, was the one chiefly used. Then, the Navajos created a secret code that was *also* used, in addition to their own Navajo language, in that war. The Navajo code contained 211 words frequently used by the military, plus an alphabet to spell out other words and proper names. This code was memorized so no time was lost and no codebooks were needed. If it seems a lot to memorize, it wasn't so bad because the codewords were associated with familiar aspects of the Navajos' peacetime lives. For example, bomber = buzzard, route = rabbit trail. Many alphabet letters were animal names; for example, A—ant—Wol-la-chee, S—sheep—Dibeh. Terms for groups of people or vehicles were graphic: a platoon was Has-dish-nih, which means mud. The Navajos using the language were called codetalkers, and most were Marines who used the code in action in the South Pacific.

SECRET WRITTEN LANGUAGES

Many kinds of ancient writing make excellent secret *written* languages. Egyptian hieroglyphics were undecipherable until the "codebook" of the Rosetta Stone was read in 1821. This is a slab of basalt inscribed by the priests of King Ptolemy V in the second century B.C. in two kinds of hieroglyphic writing and in Greek. Greek was known, and it was correctly assumed that all three versions meant the same thing. Take another look at the hieroglyphs—conventionalized pictures—in chapter 2. You can use them as part of your own hieroglyphic language.

Runes were used mainly in Scandinavia and the British Isles starting at about 300 A.D., before Christianity came to these countries. The word "rune" itself means secret. Runes can be seen in inscriptions on weapons, ornaments, and stone.

An Egyptian priest wearing a "print dress"—hieroglyphic liturgical texts

A rune stone of Sweden

Ogham, a secret language used by the Druids, developed from an Irish runic language. It can still be seen in tombstone inscriptions, chiefly in western Ireland.

Shorthand has been used as a secret written language since Roman times, because it is not only secret, but fast. In the seventeenth century, Samuel Pepys, a civil servant living in London, used shorthand to keep his diary secret. The shorthand was called Tachygraphy from the Greek "swift writing." Here are a couple of lines from the diary:

When the diary was discovered many years after Pepys' death, people thought it was in a cipher he had invented. It was only solved in the nineteenth century. Pepys wanted to be remembered as secretary of the navy—he was a very good one—but he is famous for his diary. The important thing is that the diary was secret when he needed it to be.

MAKING UP
SECRET LANGUAGES

You can even make up your own secret language. It needn't be complicated. You need some nouns and verbs, with a way of expressing the past, present, and future. You would want some descriptive words and a few common phrases and expressions.

You can also create a language using English, but you should use a secret "vocabulary" of special words and phrases known only to your group. For example, "tabby cat" could mean "meet me after school." "Striped tabby cat" could be "meet me after school at the park." Or you could start and end every word with P, or put a G between each letter, though that would make everything rather long-winded.

Many families have private codewords and phrases taken from a familiar family situation or a favorite book. In the author's family, they quote A. A. Milne's Pooh books—a word or two of a particular poem or scene is enough to describe secretly a person or a situation. Some families have a special whistle or call to each other.

Larger social groups, such as the Cockneys of London, had a very distinct lifestyle and used a special rhyming slang. For example, a man might shout to a neighbor, "My battle and strife [wife] has gone and fallen down the apples and pears [stairs]."

A phonetic "language" is easy to write, less easy to read. You write the words the way they *sound,* not the way they are *spelled.* Leaving out capitals and punctuation and running the words together improves the effect:

djoonizkummingrowndwensdeeeyempleezd

There are no limits to the new secret languages you can create.

CHAPTER ELEVEN

NONSECRET "CODES"

After all that secrecy, it's good to know that a great many codes are *not* meant to be secret. We use many of them without even thinking in our daily lives. They are written, audible, and visual, and are intended to make communication easier, quicker, cheaper, and simpler.

The computer reigns today. From the moment we are born, we get our own computer codes. Birth certificates are coded and stored in a computer, and so are social security numbers. As part of a community, we share zip codes and telephone area codes. Our automobile license plates are part of a registration code.

At the supermarket, the goods you buy are also coded. The lines and numbers on the side of a box or jar are in the Universal Product Code, which can be read by the store's computer for prices and expiration dates. The manufacturer's code is shown in the stamp you see on the bottom of cans or boxes. The Thomas J. Lipton Company date-codes its packages like this:

8CO8KF

8   stands for the year packed (1988)
C   is the month (January = A, February = B, *March*
     = C, etc.)
08   is the day
K   is the machine
F   is the plant

When you go to the library to choose a nonfiction book, you use the library's cataloging code. If you want a book on spies, you look under 327 of the Dewey Decimal System.

In business, companies save time and money by sending their cables in an international code. In the Western Union Code, whole sentences can be represented by a single word. Companies similarly abbreviate their names and addresses. An English publisher used to have the cable address BUTIBOOX LONDON. Coded abbreviations of company names are used on the stock market board.

SIGNALLING

Morse Code • One way of communicating fast is by signaling. The Morse Code is probably the best known signalling code. Morse is actually a substitution cipher with dots and dashes replacing letters. It is mostly used for telegraph messages. See the International Morse Code on page 74.

Morse can also be used visually; for example, using blinker lamps at night, with one pre-arranged sign for dot and another for dash.

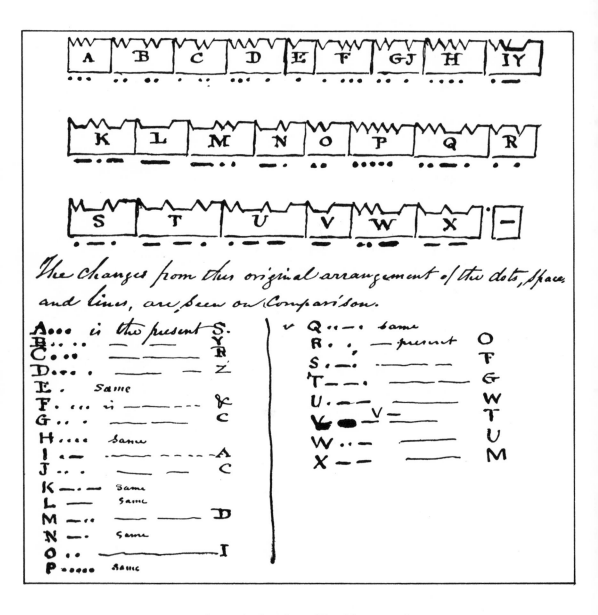

A rough drawing of the Morse code
made by Samuel Morse in 1870

A familiar signalling code is semaphore.
It uses arms in different positions to
show letters or numbers.

Semaphore • Perhaps the other most familiar signalling code is semaphore. It was much used before radio and electricity for distance signalling between ships or ship to shore. Semaphore is also a substitution cipher. It uses two levered arms with each letter or number shown by a different position of the arms. Human arms can be used too, extended by flags for visibility or flashlights in the dark.

An applied version of the semaphore code is found in railroad signalling, which uses a post and arm and colored lights. The writer Russell Hoban describes another variation of a railroad lighting code—the London Underground (subway):

> *There are six lights on the front of each train, two vertical rows of three, and the pattern in which some are lit and some are dark tells the destination. For Special Trains all six are lit. Three on the left and the bottom one on the right say Upminster and so forth.*

Other Signalling Codes • At sea, an international code of flags is used. The flags are many different shapes and colors, each representing a letter, a number, or a sentence. They are hoisted to convey messages to other ships or to shore. For example, the letter V means "I require assistance." Codebooks are in all major languages. At the office of the Federal Express courier delivery service, naval flag code stickers are used—to say "Bravo Zulu" or "job well done" about well-written reports or memos.

Fog signals use a variety of noise producers—gongs, bells, horns, whistles—to warn coastal vessels in another code of invisible dangers. For example, one long blast at two-minute intervals or less means a ship is under way.

Back on land, coded signals also figure in the way sports are directed by umpires and referees. More secretly, at a baseball game, the catcher might use prearranged hand movements to talk to the pitcher, perhaps to tell him what is happening out of his line of vision.

Truck drivers and many car drivers use the Citizens Band (CB) on the radio to talk in code to others on their wavelength. This is a real code with a codebook. The Ten Code's series of numbers stand for specific phrases, such as 10–47: EMERGENCY ROAD REPAIR NEEDED. Over 300 code terms describe life on the road. A "thermos bottle" is a tanker truck. "Bear cave" is a police station on the highway.

Ranch owners brand their cattle with special signs to show ownership. They choose their brands from a code of letters, numbers, pictures, and mathematical symbols. In Mary O'Hara's *My Friend Flicka,* a "goose" brand signified that the cattle came from the ranch called the Goose Bar.

Millions of deaf people use a complete language, known as American Sign Language (ASL), made up of hand signals and body

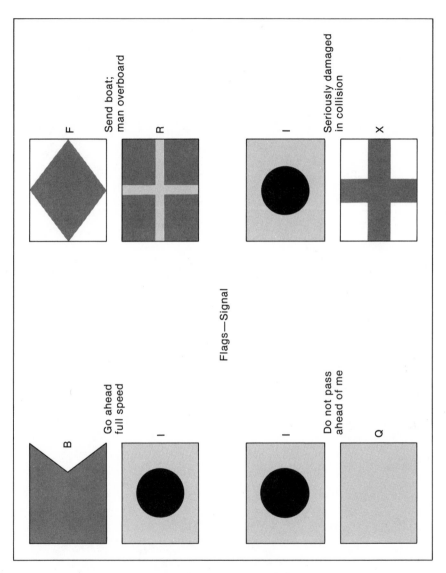

International code of flags
used at sea

Signaling from a ship during the Civil War

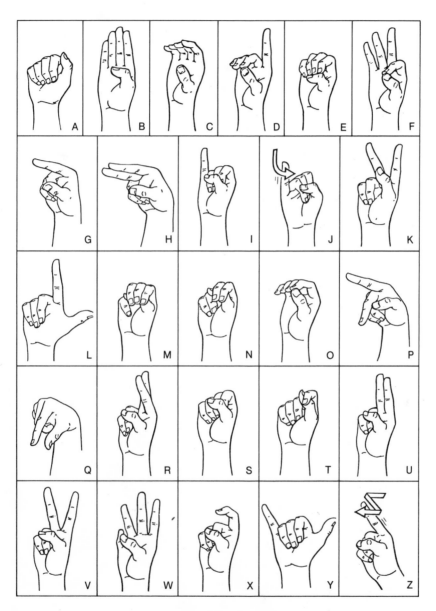

American Sign Language

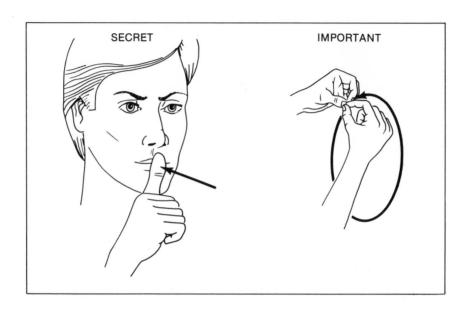

SECRET   IMPORTANT

Signing for the concepts,
"secret" and "important"

language. ASL uses concepts—for example, the signs shown here for the concepts "important" and "secret,"—and also uses a manual alphabet to spell out words letter by letter when needed. If you have seen two deaf people signing or watched a sign interpreter, you will have noticed the clear hand movements, the lips often also mouthing the words, and facial expressions helping to convey meaning. American Sign Language is rich and expressive.

Braille, the written language of the blind, is actually a substitution cipher written by means of raised dots that can be felt by the fingertips. On the next page is the Braille alphabet. You will have to imagine that the dots are raised on the page.

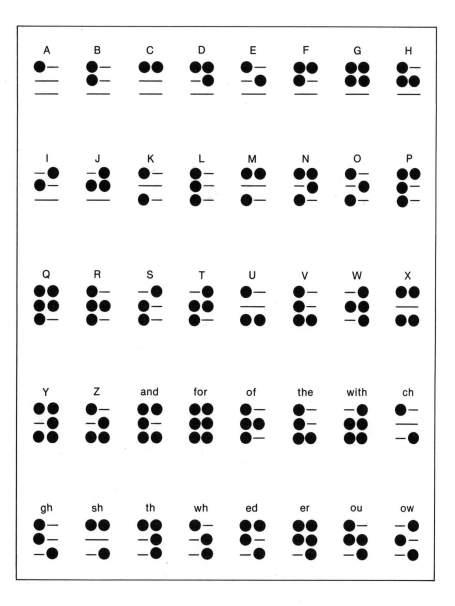

The Braille alphabet

SYMBOLS

Symbols can convey messages. A picture is often worth a thousand words . . . and often expresses an idea more clearly. The line between codes, ciphers, symbols, and signs can sometimes be blurred. It is often difficult to say where one ends and another begins. Symbols stand for or substitute for something else—words, sentences, ideas. Road signs are symbols, map information is given in symbols. The intentions are perfectly clear.

If you are in the Boy Scouts or Girl Scouts, you may be familiar with trail signs. Lord Baden-Powell, founder of the Boy Scouts, was buried in Kenya. On his grave is the scout trail sign: ◎ which means, "I have gone home."

Symbols make communication possible where cultures and languages cross, at places such as airports, railroad stations, and hotels. These symbols are coded in so far as they stand for something, but they are—or should be—clear enough for everyone to understand.

Only those in the know understand the codes of certain professions, such as mathematics, chemistry, astronomy, proofreading. Doctors, however, who used to write their prescriptions in Latin symbols are more likely nowadays to write them in plain English.

At times of upheaval in society, symbols provide powerful shorthand coded messages—secular ones such as a national flag, or religious symbols like the Christian cross and the Jewish Star of David. At a time of religious persecution in England in the seventeenth century, safe houses for Catholics on the run, such as Mapledurham in Berkshire, were identified by shell symbols glistening above a high window, discreetly visible from afar.

Road signs are symbols.

Two symbols: top, *the United Nations symbol;*
bottom, *the international symbol of the deaf.*

More recently, when President Ferdinand Marcos of the Philippines ran his last election campaign, and throughout the demonstrations that led to his overthrow, opposition supporters kept morale high with the hand signal L for *Laban* (which means "people power") just as Winston Churchill did with his V for Victory sign in the second World War.

In an extended sense, "code" also means a systematic set of laws, from the Latin "codex," meaning book. The Napoleonic Code, for example, embodies the civil law system of France.

Different societies have their own codes of behavior, and classes within those societies have rules of what is socially acceptable. Clothes convey a strong visual message. Military uniforms and civilian work clothes place people in their work hierarchy, showing where they fit into society. A dress code at school may require jackets and ties for boys and blouses and skirts for girls. Religious rituals use books, vestments, and accessories as part of a symbolic code.

Keep your eyes and ears open. Not only can you find many other nonsecret codes in your everyday life, but that loose brick in the wall or that hole in the tree may reveal a secret code or cipher that only you can solve.

Sherlock Holmes said in *The Adventure of the Dancing Men,* "What one man can invent, another can discover."

NOTE

If you wondered what Sherlock Holmes was saying in those examples we worked out, here is that part of *The Adventure of the Dancing Men:*

These hieroglyphics have evidently a meaning. If it is a purely arbitrary one, it may be impossible for us to solve it. If, on the other hand, it is systematic, I have no doubt that we shall get to the bottom of it. But this particular sample is so short that I can do nothing and the facts which you have brought me are so indefinite that we have no basis for an investigation. I would suggest that you return to Norfolk . . . and that you take an exact copy of any further dancing men which may appear. . . .

I have here in front of me these singular productions, at which one might smile, had they not proved themselves to be the forerunners of so terrible a tragedy. I am fairly familiar with all forms of secret writings and am myself the author of a trifling monograph upon the subject in which I analyze 160 separate ciphers, but I confess that this is entirely new to me. The object of those who invented the system has apparently been to conceal that these characters convey a message. Having once recognized that the symbols stood for letters and having applied the rules which guide us in all forms of secret writings, the solution was easy enough. The first message submitted to me was so short that it was impossible for me to do more than say, with some confidence, that this symbol stood for E. . . .

Want to know the rest of the story? You can read it for yourself in *The Complete Sherlock Holmes* or another collection of the works of Sir Arthur Conan Doyle.

FOR FURTHER READING

Bielewicz, Julian A. *Secret Languages: Communicating in Codes and Ciphers.* New York: Elsevier-Nelson, 1976.

Cohen, Daniel. *The Science of Spying.* New York: McGraw-Hill, 1977.

Epstein, Sam, and Epstein, Beryl. *The First Book of Codes and Ciphers.* New York: Franklin Watts, 1956.

Garden, Nancy. *The Kids' Code and Cipher Book.* New York: Holt, Rhinehart and Winston, 1981.

Haswell, Jock. *Spies and Spymasters: A Concise History of Intelligence.* London: Thames and Hudson, 1977.

Janeczko, Paul B. *Loads of Codes and Secret Ciphers.* New York: Macmillan, 1984.

Kahn, David. *The Code-breakers.* New York: Macmillan, 1967.

———. *Kahn on Codes: Secrets of the New Cryptology.* New York: Macmillan, 1983.

Sarnoff, Jane and Ruffins, Reynold. *The Code and Cipher Book.* New York: Scribner, 1975.

Wolfe, James R. *Secret Writing: The Craft of the Cryptographer.* New York: McGraw-Hill, 1970.

Zim, Herbert S. *Codes and Secret Writing.* New York: Morrow-Scholastic Book Services, 1948. Reprinted, 1970.

INDEX

ABOUT
THE AUTHOR

KARIN MANGO grew up in
Reading, England, and published
her first book at age fourteen.
She has since published ten
other books, including fiction
for young adults and nonfiction
for the junior high age group.
She received her M.A. from
Edinburgh University in Scotland,
and an M.L.S. from Pratt Institute.
She and her family live in a
brownstone with a garden in
Brooklyn, New York.